Windows To The Soul

Seeing Clearly...

INSPIRATIONAL POEMS, REFLECTIONS AND WRITINGS

DYORA THOMAS-KINSEY

WINDOWS TO THE SOUL
COPYRIGHT © 2024 BY DYORA THOMAS-KINSEY

Contents

Introduction

"Windows to The Soul...Seeing Clearly" is the first of a three-book series. The collection of poems was written over years of self-scrutiny and wondering how I was so different from others. Looking with new eyes, I contemplated and realized it could be that I revealed too much about myself while other people only tell the highlights of their successes. As I looked through this lens and my focus widened, I saw that others make mistakes too, but may not be inclined to reveal them so readily. This book, focuses on everyday encounters with others, finding a deeper observation and understanding without comparisons.

Not a psychologist or therapist, I consider myself an introspective individual who decided to share these totally inspired writings. I credit my grandparents, parents, and so many others involved in my spiritual growth who helped me through difficult times. I don't know how people survive if they don't have a higher power in God to hand their problems to when they don't have answers.

Truth in poetry, for me, started out as teardrops and rips in countless piles of paper. I had to first get out the hurt and anger. Then came a word. Then words, a sentence, a paragraph, and eventually, stringing those words into a poem. Those first poems addressed what I saw and felt in comparison with what I lacked. At that time, people other than myself represented an incredulous life that made me feel small and constantly caused me to self-analyze. I then started to widen my focus to discover what was really true.

Your Little Boy

I'll always be your little boy,
Today, tomorrow, and evermore.

No matter your job, what you feel you need,
I'm here. Please see me.

I need a man nearby to help shape my life.
A father is great, but a good male friend is more than alright.

To see and compare is a necessary must.
I'm not saying you can't do it, but I'm learning to notice, to
trust

That we are very different in how we were made.
I must truly appreciate my body, that little boy mind that
starts to fade.

I study your answers, how you protect me like a soft shell.
Let me see a from man's viewpoint how he handles life as
well.

There is room in my life for both a man and you.
Let me make up my mind, when I'm grown, which path I'll
choose.

The Protector

I hold in my hands
My future, my fate.
How I look at life
Drives the path I take.

Mom raised me, Dad gave me
All the basics I needed
Together, they did their best,
And now, it's up to me.

The circumstances of my life,
The episodes I've lived,
Everything that's come to pass,
Both bad and then good.

They helped shape my character
And the one I've now become.
I want to show the world my person,
As I'm measured by all I've done.

Excuses, should I have them,
Are all mine to bear.
Blaming Mom and Dad is lame
And really just isn't fair.

I'm grown, know better. I know
What society will take.
Wasting life away is foolish.
I had to put on the brakes.

When family stops helping as a crutch
And leaves a loved one out to rot,
You might doubt and say "Why me?
Why was I born to this lot?"

Next comes the questions,
All you did or didn't do.
Can you help yourself do better?
And then help your family improve?

Did family forsake one person
Only to support the whole?
Was it preservation you perceived?
Has your life lost the ultimate goal?

"There's always one who comes forward," said Dad.
"One to support, take chances, answer the call.
Back the one who will protect family,
For they will ultimately protect us all."

Insight

Every action brings a reaction.
Every reaction brings a consequence.
Consequence can also be seen as importance.
To be important is to be significant.

Significant people have influence.
To have influence is to have authority.
To have authority, in many instances,
Is to have power over peers, over many.
Power over peers is best won through knowledge.

Have you ever wondered
If you are intellectually knowledgeable
Or simply,
Successfully clever?

It's About Me

I wanna do coke, it's all about me.
I wanna drag smoke, just please let me be.

I wanna eat food, all I can eat.
I'm in a funky mood, hell, it's all about me.

I'm gonna have sex, 'cause it feels good.
I'm gonna be the man, 'cause I know I'm good.

I'm gonna deck you, just 'cause I can, man.
I'm gonna do the do, 'cause I am the man.

Get offa me cop, don't touch me!
You hurtin' my arm, gimme a break please!

You clubbed my head, but I got rights here!
I say I'm hurtin' now, but you don't see my fear.

My pad is jail now, gave me life for drugs.
They say that fool Mac identified my mug.

That sorry homie just turned me in.
Deacon Jones says, "It was all about sin."

Been long years here, but it now makes sense.
Even prison guards say I was plain dense.

No one took the time to explain to me
The permanent pull of this whole gang thing.

My family tried at times to bring me back.
Mama often cried, but I was numb to facts.

I was seven when the gang took me in.
I learned to please me, to be loyal to them.

Gangs were safe, thought no one hurts them.
Dares were met, numbers would always win.

Never go alone, we learned the smart way.
Cops ignored the Hood, and we learned to play.

That's how I learned to please me, be me.
That's how I learned to do coke, smoke dope.

That's why I'm in here, why I know fear.
It's too late for me. They won't release anytime near.

Don't wanna do coke, drag smoke.
Don't wanna eat food, be in a good mood.

There's no play, I've got little say.
Just be stone cold and have no soul.

So, preacher, see me and help me!
Take my words out there! They must care!

My brothers hurt and die here, just lie here.
Death and evil are here, so there is fear!

Don't wanna do coke,
No smoke.

Don't wanna eat food,
No mood.

Don't wanna have sex,
Nor deck.

Man, I failed me,
'Cause it was all about me.

Are You Smart?

Intelligence
is a relative notion,
for you see,
it all depends on
if you can comprehend
the pertinent facts.
Then, if you can recall them,
recall them only to those
who want
to hear.

Old Habits

Dragging on a cigarette,
contemplations unknown.
Looking malnourished,
sad, very obviously alone.

He stares at the corn
which seems miles away.
Thoughts are hidden from others,
those who don't know his name.

Does he have a job
to keep him occupied?
Does he have a life
to keep him satisfied?

Clothes hanging off his body,
neat yet baggy against the thin frame within.
His leg, perched on the porch banister
to anchor the palm which cups his chin.

Longing to say a word or two,
to show someone who really cares.
She's afraid to break his solitude.
To intrude in his thoughts, she doesn't dare.

He flicks the cigarette and turns away,
goes down the steps, then to his car.
She watches closely as he speeds down the road.
"I care," she says, but he's gone too far.

Professional

They may hire you as a professional
For all they want you to do,
They may pay a six-figure salary
And give you all you so choose.

Processes and procedures, always fair game.
After all, job progress is what most expect.
Back brief, give credit for what others do right,
As nothing in the workplace is ever flawless.

Just don't be drawn in as an informant or a spy
For those with whom you pretend to share trust.
And don't undermine allegiances you've sought.
Don't talk of dealings with others in disgust.

Take care you don't lose a friendship
Or damage an employee's ability to confide,
For your integrity stays with you for a lifetime.
A breach of it, any breach, will weigh forever on your mind

No Such Thing

There is no such thing as
...good luck
...a bad-seed child
...bad karma
...a dependable politician
...an alien abduction
...a good beating
...an acceptable racial slur

There is no such thing as
...a perfect body
...happy blues
...a half-truth
..."I didn't mean to say that"
...the fountain of youth
...forever in your debt
...a pet tiger
...a contented prisoner
...a guiltless murder

There is no such thing as
...a one-night-stand girlfriend
...just a little pregnant
...a well-meaning frenemy

...all of this is true

The Color Of Woman

What is the color of woman
who fights for equality?
Why does she want my job, my status?
What are those stated inequities?

"I am the color red."
"The protective core of my family."
"All its pain, all its joy,
the nurturer, yes. That is me."

"I am the color yellow."
"The warmth from which things grow, all that you see."
"My influence can make the coldest things melt.
Benevolence, that's me."

"I am the color white."
"Seeking knowledge, I've always known that was the key."
"Self-assured, I know life will flourish."
"This confidence in me is all you should see."

"I am the color black."
"The strength from which all life survives,
Prevailing through sorrow with my Heavenly guide,
the great survivor am I."

"Blend these together, and I am your rainbow
From whence your answers will come."
"Stay with me just a moment longer.
You'll understand once I'm done."

"I am the rainbow of your hopes,
the rainbow of your dreams, your desires."
"I am made from parts of you,
so I have the same burning fires."

"Acknowledge our hopes, acknowledge our dreams,
and acknowledge our similar desires."
"Walk with me for equality,
and you will be that much more admired."

"But don't forget that I am the shades,
Red, yellow, white, and black."
"I am your blended rainbow of color.
Now, let us fight for equality, and all that's right."

Supporting My Turn

What kind of rights do women have as wives,
As many men berate and tear down their lives?
Many Wives don't care what other people say or do,
But some are kept in the dark and don't even have a clue.

They trust their man's word, "He'll care for us."
Pensions and insurance their men say are a must.
Wives' names are on the documents, they tell them so,
Everything is done, should their mate prematurely go.

Military Services tries to help with SBP.
"Survivors Benefit Plan is what they want to give me."
Military members pay into the plan,
And to deny it, as beneficiary, I must sign.

"It is my chance to decide
if I want this plan at this specific time,
Something that individually protects me,
Yes, this will definitely be all mine."

The briefing an hour long, explains it all.
"My spouse must attend. He doesn't want me to stall."
He squirms and hates the fact he's not in control.
SBP is not in his future plans, oh no, not one of his goals.

"That money is thrown away and goes to the bad.
I've investments and insurance, so this plan makes me mad.

I'll go to the top and change it all if I can,
No one can make us select this plan!"

"Just give me a chance, honey, please let me see.
This plan's meant for me, so let me evaluate please."
He feels mistrust after all he's been through.
"Why can't you blindly trust me? I know just what to do."

He tells his office workers, who can't believe what they hear.
"She did what to you? Did we hear you clear?"
"We told you what to do, brought you reading stuff"
"She embarrassed you there?" They were all in a huff.

So, when he gets home, with all his rekindled anger,
He tells of his office staff. This annoys her further,
Makes her feel small for having doubts and sharing them.
Manipulated cruelty when it was never about him.

Why can't she take time, to reach her own conclusions?
It will probably the same as his but this is her decision.

He won't take time, and his threats make her think,
"Trust me now, or else. We should always be in sync."

Locked in and secure, he's not thinking down the road.
Many men leave wives in order to have a younger one in their
abode.
His wife recalls past threats; even now, it makes her think.
If they part ways in the future, her security is gone in a blink.

That's why this plan is for spouses.
He doesn't have to pay out the nose.
Agree on a dollar lesser amount for her?
No one wants to step on toes.
"Honey, just let me feel secure,
I can't lose you and everything else
And then, to tell your office folk
makes me feel exposed as hell."

"Pressure of this issue is less than what's fair to me
All I see is me and the kids out there, somewhere I don't want
to be,
So give me a chance. Believe in me, give me some facts to help
me think.
You are my partner, show me don't scold me. Then, we can
be truly in sync."

Leader

We've had the solution all along.
It was right under our nose.

Come together as a force of one,
Where not everyone is a foe.

To get anywhere, there must be belief
That one is sincere, that one understands.

One must identify with the plight of many.
One must demonstrate a fix they have at hand.

Now, watch that person with an eagle eye,
All talk, no show are the keys.

To keep disappointment from the masses of men,
Give power only if they show interest in you and me.

Military And Alone

Sometimes, it's nearly impossible
To keep it all cherished and together.
The passion, the desire is recognized.
How loneliness can make one feel so desperate,

So much so, you avoid all persons, all things
That might tempt your loins or needs.
You think you'll go mad as you throb and pray
The desire be taken far away from me.

To stay true to your love who's fighting a war,
You ask, "What profession" has such a burden as we?
Do they know what they ask of our love, of me?
Can you understand why that must be?

Is it natural for spouses to part for so long,
As thoughts turn to such feverish aches?
So much they're fought down continually,
The mind never giving you any break.

To fight the label of Jezebel or Cad
For one mistake in loss of self-control...
While the military parts couples with extended duty,
That community must bond tightly, must uphold.

As a link in a group of dialogue and activities,
When their soldier is away, a duty call,
Their only defense is group prayer, group faith.
Spouses encourage each one not to drop the ball.

Families must be as solid as our fighting force
Who do their jobs in spite of political sides.
Soldiers need support from communities at home
Who are ready to defend our nation without compromise.

So let our military men and women know
You care for them, that they are not alone.
When you thank them for their service,

thank their families too,
For their sacrifices are what keep us all
safe in our homes.

Tears Of Freedom

Freedom makes me want to cry great tears
For those who suffer, fighting, dying, facing such fears,
Heroes present and past who detest unfair opposition.
Their stubborn resolve is what I truly owe to my position.

Remembering my ancestors and stories told and untold,
Their quest for freedom is why each tale unfolds.
No matter how I got here are in terms of my birth,
They never emphasize sorrow, rather celebration and mirth.

And what of other such heroes amongst us today,
Reacting in the face of trouble, the strong, the foreigner, the gay.
Whatever their position, they act, not just quarrel.
They help those in danger, no matter their personal peril.

So regardless of how your rivals hurt you. And yes, your
rivals will.
They resent your situation, and for that, they may kill.
They'll try to stamp out your willpower, a definite must,
Since it's not always money that causes their disgust.

Thus, recollect occasionally how innocence will fall
With those present tyrants who cause masses to be appalled.
There are heroes past and present who face uncertainty and
fear.
Please be brave, honor their greatness, swallow those tears.

Valuables

Life is precious.
Babies are precious.
Health is precious too.

Honor is precious.
Integrity is precious.
Mores are held deeply as true.

Money is hoarded.
Oil is hoarded.
Excess food is stored for future use.

Resources are hoarded
For those who can afford them,
So much in the world kept for so few.

At What Price?

The longer
You seem to
Know a person

And the more
Endeared
You become

The more you learn
To dislike
Their ways

To fear permanent
Damage
To be done

Just review
All of those
Characteristics

That drew you in
So close
To them

Then, realize
No one
Is perfect

And strive
To fall in love
Once again

Yesterdays

He chose to hang on to his yesterdays
With childlike laughter and quite simple games.
So very far from perfect surroundings,
Thinking nothing would really harm him.

A strange mixture of neighbors, some Polish,
Some Black, many mixed cultures, words and taboos.
All people, thrown together by nothing more than shared
destitution.
Hurting a child was something none would ever do.

Uneven sidewalks, one of the only great dangers
Of running, tripping then, slamming your head.
And of course, you never ventured more than a mile
Since you had to mind even what Grandpa said.

Penny candies and cinnamon money chews,
None packaged but all safe to eat.
Don't worry if you don't have the right amount of change.
Mr. Charlie will say "take it." Oh wow, he was neat!

Self-esteem at an all-time high,
No dating or kissing at all thought of.
Just being with those who interested you most,
Who shared your cares, most of all, your sports loves.

Is it possible to have more yesterdays
With all its uncomplicated fun?
No cunning, no eyeing that sabotaging fool,
No preoccupation with the round you just won.

Can this be the true reason a few successful ones
Just quit their jobs and head for the hills?
To live the rest of their thoughtful yesterdays
Through the present privacy they have built?

He chose to hang on to his yesterdays
With childlike laughter and quite simple games.
An isolated place with poor, simple surroundings.
He smiles now. He is so glad he came.

Broken Family

The middle-class family was fortunate.
Kids had loving parents who cared.
They took in the children of others
When many similar would not have dared.

God blessed them with a long life of happiness
And grandchildren who grew up with the same,
So what has gone wrong with the family now
Who haven't much in common but their name?

Did anyone monitor kids' surroundings growing up,
How they treated each other when they were alone?
How about the perception of a parent's favorite child?
Did all truly feel loved at home?

Was there any kind of inappropriate play
These children tried to warn the parents about?
Between themselves or between grown-ups?
Did the parents act harshly or meanly voice their doubts?

Did the parents give time to each child,
And let them know they too were special?
Or were expectations and knowledge compared,
Making the kids feel their parents were partial?

Can anyone understand such a giant rift,
One that might tear a family apart?
Hurt kids don't really know how to love themselves,
So how can they figure this one out?

Some say, "Let those kids mature.
Then, may they have children of their own.
Insulate those grandkids from perceived fears."
But children often imitate what they see and hear…

Healing starts with the older ones, those now grown,
Those who are insecure, somewhat fragile, in need of support.
No matter the success or money these adults have,
Such practices are a losing battle defending a falling fort.

Cutting ties with family one really loves
Definitely hurts everyone in the end.
All must talk through their hatred, shame, or hurt,
For family will always, always be kin.

Parents have sacrificed and done everything they can
to push their grown adults together again.
No one can just make them communicate,
Now it is simply now up to them.

They're grown now and have lives of their own.
They'll reflect, we hope, on how to do things.
Just pray they forgive both themselves and their family
For the mistakes so common to all human beings.

Who Are You

Who are you that you go to dine
With my mom and my dad tonight?
How do you know the importance of their wishes?
How have you stayed friends so tight?

What are your dreams and personal thoughts,
All you share with each other so dear?
Tell us the secret! What is the glue
That has bonded you so across all these years?

Our generation has somehow lost
The gift you all carefully hold.
Or was it the hard times of struggles and pain
Which you worked through, due to these friends of gold?

We enjoyed life around the world
But forgot we needed to come home.
The ones my age were given the best,
So we felt all could be solved over the phone.

"Inventions are good," we tell ourselves,
"Improvements get better when refined."
We sadly forget that there are people we leave behind,
Lost bonding felt over time.

So where will that leave us in the future,
When the aged eventually need assistance?
Do you hire someone or leave a companion,
As others selfishly enjoy their distance?

Who are you that go to dine
With my mom and my dad tonight?
They are friends and family who take up the slack.
So, reward them on sight, please don't fight.

Stepchild Anger

Why do you hate me?
I'm the one who needs attention.
You've taken away my father.
I'm entitled to this temper tantrum!

My world is a hot mess.
Won't someone just think of me?
You have the wonderful life.
There is so little for me to see.

You judge me from your world of comfort
And see me as project torn trash.
Because you were met with initial resistance,
You label me as tainted, hardcore, bad.

I didn't ask to be here at all.
How I was raised isn't mine or yours to recall.
As a stepmom you can make things easier or not,
But my mom and dad are truly all that I've got.

Don't make me choose between you and her.
She gave me life; I've known her forever.
That has to, of course, count for something,
So don't call my mom and me good for nothing.

You are the adult, not me just yet.
If I rejected you in the past, don't hold me to that debt.
Can't you see my pain, my many cries for help?
Stop thinking of only you, your uncomfortable self!

Help me love my dad, even still,
Even though he left me and my mom of his free will.
Just try to see things from my point of view:
I am suffering, feeling pain. Good times are so few.

I am worth it, have faith. Just you wait and see.
I can't reach you right now, for you give up too easily,
But I know I'm not a fool. I just don't know the right tools.
I want my dad to love me, to reach out again please.

I maybe a bit immature,
Though I won't fully accept that now.
My world has been turned upside down.
I don't really care who won any sort of round.

Just please help my family mend our hearts.
I can't do it myself, I need some relief.
Embrace us all, not just my dad.
If you ask me for help, that's a good place to start.

We Need You

Brother, we always need you sober
To keep the kids from drinking.
Identify with them, give them hope.
Help them kick the bad habit, as you did.

Brother, we need you drug-free.
Warn all our folk against that trap.
Talk against the first hit.
Convince them, please, to stay off that crap.

Brother, we need you free from anger,
To teach love, forgiveness, tolerance.
Help keep kids free from all the killing,
from being dangerous, give-them-no-chance menaces.

Brother, we need you in a life free from envy.
So many resent what others have.
Help to encourage hard work and integrity,
To inspire a planned goal with a definite path.

Flaunt your education and knowledge, my brother,
Let us show teens and adolescents a positive thing.
Take the time to read a book.
Show by example! Let them see your personal dream.

We need you to reach them now,
We'll make our rich brothers accountable to help.
They'll set the stage and path for your escape
when you're ready to work hard, yourself.

It's essential for you to want to change.
We need you to climb out of the near-poverty cage,
To encourage children to do the same thing.
Help us stop the tirade of killing and rage.

Brother, we need you to trust once again,
to help us form a solid, strong core.
We're too fractured and weak from revenge.
Let us please find some way to make amends.

My turn, Brother. The kids need both you and me
To open their eyes. Can't those rich folk, see?
They're experienced in dealing with money,
But we've had the survival-instinct journey.

Open eyes will help stave off annihilation.
We have the remnants of a splintered yet noble nation.
Help us survive and carry on our presence.
We're the vestiges of a deeply historic civilization.

The conquered tactic was classically unfortunate,
the outside-smiling winner pitted you against me.
The fighting remains implanted within our selves.
Sadly, we've become the foe we must rally and beat.

The ammo are drugs, alcohol, no jobs, deceitful fun.
Add hopelessness and the damage is nearly done.
Make brothers hallucinate, then give them guns.
With judgment gone, nearly everyone wants to run.

Well, the old cannot continue to flee,
and the hot-headed young have failed see.
The broke-down families are replaced by crooks,
and they stress results as a successful key and hook.

Tell our rich brothers we must fight covert discrimination
on the grounds where it is most deeply embedded.
It's in our minds and against our own kind,
a hatred for our own is why we've stumbled and shredded.

Listen, if you can make a bird think he's a favored bird,
turn him against his own and prime other birds for cooking.
Then, tell him he's changed and isn't a bird at all.
He'll change his ways and help you with the bird-looking.

That's why we need you, and you need me.
Individually, each puzzle piece, we separately see.
Just think of the impact to be made,
if we work together,
think how many lives can be truly saved.

Brother, let's be smart. I may not be rich, but I know facts.
Let's meet together in a mutual pact,
merge survival instincts with money as our sure bet.
We need economic power to change laws and gain more
respect.

We need programs to deprogram today's harmful thinking.
Let's get rich brothers to assist us, to keep us all from sinking.
There are some of us who want to choose the best track.
Don't sell us out now! Help us reinforce our encumbered
backs!

Parenting

The hardest thing about parenting
Is learning when to let the grown kids go.
The lessons kids learn, the choices they make
Can sometimes feel like bad blow after bad blow.

Protection or acceptance is what parents must decide upon,
While walking the faulty path young kids may choose.
Will parents discipline or make kids pay the price?
Should they shelter them or make them lose

The freedom of choice they've so learned to enjoy?
Everyone makes decisions though trial and error.
Yet, there's a narrow band of risks and acceptance,
For no one wants loved ones to be exposed to danger.

Young people test limits of society,
Though we hope they do it when they are young.
How will parents know when to draw the line
When mistakes often outweigh one simple wrong?

It is so painful disciplining any growing kid,
As they must learn the rules and then obey.
Laws must be followed while we protect kids from harm,
And we remind them of that day after day after day.

Weighing the penalties of terrible behavior,
We should let kids experience some pain.
The lessons learned foster responsibility,
So we can control of ourselves and still remain sane

The longer you let kids put off accountability
Makes them think they can fully get away
Manipulating strings, performing wrongdoings, it's okay.
They'll never learn to comply with the establishment's way.

Raising a kid with shaky morals and behavior
Is sadly what some parents have done.
Shielding a child who is prone to break the law
With no penalties makes a hardened daughter or son.

Who said raising children was easy
And the hardest time was the birth?
From the moment they were conceived up until now,
A parent's instinct is to protect them from all hurt.

An unlearned lesson is what kids will face later,
Consequences seen then as an adult,
All because their parents failed to let them face
An earlier hand they themselves dealt.

But parents must face reality!
No matter how each kid is raised,
They hopefully try to do their best.
For bad choices force everyone to pay.

Finding guilt in yesterday's harmful choices
Is like water flowing swiftly beneath a bridge.
What's done is done, but it's not totally up to them.
Reflect on how to redirect that growing kid!

Pay now or later, that's the certainty.
This is how society's kids truly learn;
Embarrassment or pain is a small price to pay,
Rather than detention or, later, living on the run

Understanding Daddy

I remember you, Daddy, in very endearing ways:

Your bear hugs, laughs, back rubs, smiles
I needed your approval each and every day.

Always scrubbing my ankles and wrists,
Soaking hours in a tub it seemed,
I did my best until dirt and dead skin had gone away.

My siblings were tough,
though I know they loved me.
As the only girl of four, we often had our rivalries.

Don't know how I was so blind
To any of their angry times.
I just needed Daddy's love for my rough days.

Some say you were hard
As a teacher in school,
While you prepared college students for lives in the military,

Years later I was told,
You did strike gold,
Teaching wisdom and truth that many did behold.

I looked to you and reviewed

Parental decisions I made, all the ways
I over-compensated for my mistakes.

And, sometimes I didn't see
All that my spouse did see,
But I observed and thanked God, for an attentive mate.

I also saw you and Mother interact,
How you communicated together
That helped me to better my kids and my own ways.

Though tangible possessions
And money brought you some pleasure,
Your greatest forte and endearing trait was simply you.

The lengths you would go to lessen life's pain
And the depths of tough sacrifice
You gave for what you believed

You were attentive, counseled needy souls,
Taught opportunity, love, honor…
That's the gift all should ultimately see.

There aren't many men
Who are heads of household and would give
Of their hearts as you did, so generously.

So, I can think of nothing else
A love-filled daughter can present to you
But love and acceptance, unconditionally.

Though others may try
To tarnish the memory of my dad,
No one but God could ever part you from me.

Thus, as months turn to years,
As decades fly by, I am patient
As I work on our lineage, our family tree.

I must also leave a written legacy
For others to clearly see:
My perspective on life with my Daddy.

Legacy Of A Name

To be a winner in life
Or in any other game,
You must first establish some kind
Of personal pride in your personal name.

Your name should reflect integrity,
Morals, self-control.
It really is a tall order,
But essential for reaching any goal.

Guide your future by accomplishments
Achieved in each moment.
Your actions are embedded in people's minds,
Through both large and small events.

There will be definite setbacks,
Disappointments along the way.
But challenge yourself to keep going
Day after day after day.

There will be people you'll forget
In less than five minutes,
While some will recall you
With good or bad judgements.

So, hold love, charity, improvement
As intangible goals very actively sought.
Your name, I say, is your legacy,
And that's all any of us have really got.

A Poem For My Mother

Mother, how do I give back to you
And let you know all I appreciate most?
Wisdom, pride, sacrifice and happy times,
A childhood of which I can now boast.

Teacups of porcelain, life-sized baby dolls,
Day camps, church camps, Campfire Girls.
Ballet and flute, you dressed me so cute,
Makeup, your high heeled shoes, making me feel tall.

From youth to adolescence, I had willful independence,
A stage that nearly all teens go through.
My self-sought attention, shocked crisis, your interventions,
Those hated lectures of yours which left me so tense.

Comparisons between me and all you did.
Those are truths I see now through my life experiences.
I never listened or heeded any advice you would give,
Though now those reflections offer great answers for my kids.

I so loathed that phrase "I told you so,"
Yet laughingly, those words now come from me.
Should I swallow my pride and confide
In that wise and eloquent mom from years ago?

Well, it only took Daddy to tell me he loved me
And the sense of urgency to confess to you, Mom.
He said, "While she is alive, it will boost her pride
To know you cared and thought her wise."

I've always loved you, Mother, in all your wisdom.
Kids' needs are different, I see that now.
So please, ignore any past spoiled whims
For all the sibling attention I felt you gave them.

I feel blessed, I have love,
I have Jesus, I have joy,
And, I have your love
Which I know you will always send.

Helping Hands

Family interaction
Is an important one.
It's very hard work,
Work that's never really done.

Things appear unfair to the oldest,
The one burdened with responsibility,
Especially when younger ones at home
Need an example to see.

Dad wonders of his carefully laid theory.
Will it ever really work?
Or will it be a failed guess
He'll quickly have to abort?

The plan is strict and diligent work,
All foundations and values he thinks are best.
He'll include wife, kids, others under his care.
Then, he'll demand lifelong family-ness.

Soon, he'll have another resource:
Teaching others down the line.
Mentoring his standards and family views,
For kid siblings explain better and often take more time.

Joy engulfs and overwhelms him
When he sees the oldest girl solve a math equation.
Then, sitting close by, involved in the process,
Is the confused but willing young son.

Tears of joy he won't let spill from his eyes,
Due to the next generational impassioned scene.
Two grandchildren with their father, explaining math problems.
Wow! What a beautiful team!

Tough Love

Listen closely
to all I have to say.

It is out of this deep love for you
that I want you to listen today.

As long as there is breath in my body
and you are under my care,
you'll live with me and your dad.

Until you are eighteen,
we'll stick together like honey and bear.

It's unfortunate we have to move now,
and you think this is where you want to be.

But a family that respects and cares for each other
works through tough times. That's just reality.

I'm proud of your many sound decisions,
that you're nearly grown and ready to leave home.

So please, dear, take this time to contemplate.
Have fun, for you'll soon be living on your own.

About The Author

Dyora Thomas-Kinsey is an enthusiastic writer and author who has experienced many diverse populations and cultures. She has lived in Japan and various cities in the United States her entire life as she has been associated with the military in different roles. All necessitated a skill in observance and inclusion to thrive and intermingle into many societies. Dyora saw the need to be proactive to ensure employment viability with the many military relocations she and her family encountered.

She first earned a Bachelor of Arts and Sciences in Interdisciplinary Studies and Dietetics, then was commissioned as an officer in the military. After her time as a military officer and receipt of a Master of Arts in Human Relations/Management, Dyora earned a teaching certificate and taught pre-kindergarten through college students. As a certified mediator and employment as an investigator with the State of Nebraska in Equal Employment Opportunity (EEO) and Housing and with the Federal EEO Program, Dyora gained valuable experience. She has over twenty-five years of knowledge, skill and experience with the federal government and several years in the civilian sector.

"Windows To the Soul, Seeing Clearly" are poems that address both the introspective and outward look into many situations as individuals attempt to both meld and assist others blend successfully into society.